Lost Railways of County Donegal
by Stephen Johnson

Railway Station, Pettigo

Text © Stephen Johnson, 2008
First published in the United Kingdom, 2008,
reprinted 2013
by Stenlake Publishing Ltd.
www.stenlake.co.uk
ISBN 9781840334272

The publishers regret that they cannot supply
copies of any pictures featured in this book.

Gweebarra Bridge.

INTRODUCTION

Donegal is a remote but beautifully scenic and mountainous county of low population. It boasted two of the best-known narrow-gauge systems in Ireland, the County Donegal Railways Joint Committee (the largest narrow-gauge company in Ireland) and the Londonderry & Lough Swilly Railway.

Although the Finn Valley Railway, West Donegal Railway and the Londonderry & Lough Swilly Railway had built some lines in the county, further building was assisted with the passing of the Light Railways (Ireland) Act of 1889, which established the principle of state aid. However, it was the Railways (Ireland) Act in 1896 that really expanded the railways, in particular the Londonderry & Lough Swilly. The provisions of this Act saw the government being in a position to almost entirely pay for new railways to open up underdeveloped and impoverished areas. The Letterkenny & Burtonport Extension Railway was just one of these lines.

The traditional traffic flows from Co. Donegal to Londonderry, the nearest large city, were severely affected with the partition of Ireland in 1922. Customs posts between the two states delayed services and despite being the most northerly county in Ireland, Donegal is in Éire and naturally an alteration in politics and trade followed. The upsurge of road transport also affected the railways despite some innovative economies, particularly the introduction of internal combustion powered railcars on the County Donegal Railways Joint Committee from 1926. The Lough Swilly didn't fair so well and started to cease services on lines from 1931, putting its efforts in road transport. The war years stemmed the tide for a while, but the post-war period saw a rapid decline in fortunes. The Lough Swilly had gone by 1953 with the County Donegal following in 1960.

The origins of the County Donegal Railways Joint Committee started with the broad-gauge Finn Valley Railway (FVR) running from Strabane to Stranorlar. The FVR was involved with another company, the West Donegal Railway, which built a 3ft. narrow-gauge line to Donegal. The companies merged, with the FVR re-gauging to 3ft. gauge, to form the Donegal Railway Company (DR). Further expansion ensued with lines built to Killybegs, Glenties, Ballyshannon and Letterkenny.

The English Midland Railway was keen to expand its interests in Ireland and consequently acquired the Belfast & Northern Counties Railway in 1903. Further expansion of the Midland Railway saw an offer made to purchase the DR. The dominant company in this area of the country was the Great Northern Railway of Ireland (GNR(I)), which made objections to the offer. Eventually a compromise was made where both companies would jointly purchase and operate the DR. Government approval for this came through on 1 May 1906 and the company subsequently became known as the County Donegal Railways Joint Committee (CDRJC).

1926 saw an interesting turn of events for the railway. In 1906 a four-wheel petrol-driven inspection vehicle had been purchased. However, in 1926 a shortage of coal due to a miners' strike saw it being used to carry mail. Pleased with the success of the vehicle, Henry Forbes, the CDRJC General Manager, thought about the possibility of using larger petrol vehicles for passenger work. Two such vehicles were acquired from the Derwent Valley Light Railway in England, re-gauged and put to work. Success with these vehicles led to the fleet being expanded until, in 1930, the first diesel-powered railcar was purchased, making it the first such vehicle to be used in the British Isles. Over the years, further diesel railcars were purchased and the railway settled to an operation using railcars for passenger work and steam engines for freight and heavy excursion traffic. The larger railcars were also able to haul trailer cars and vans. The fact that railcars were easier to stop than steam engines also resulted in a number of extra stops being provided between stations, at level crossings and other places; in fact just about anywhere there were passengers.

Unlike other railways in the newly formed Irish Free State, during the 1920s the CDRJC managed to escape amalgamation into the Great Southern Railways as a result of its joint ownership by the GNR(I) and the Midland Railway (later the London, Midland & Scottish Railway). The line saw a brief period of profitability during the Second World War with increased traffic; however, the overall trend in the decline in profitability had already been set by the late 1930s and resumed with the return to peace. Falling traffic on the Glenties line saw it being the first victim, closing to passengers in 1947.

Another problem occurred with the nationalisation of the British railway system in 1948. The London Midland Region of the newly formed British Railways now owned half of the CDRJC. This was subsequently transferred to the Ulster Transport Authority (UTA) upon the formation of that concern, also in 1948. The 1950s saw a downturn in the fortunes of the GNR(I), by 1953 jointly run by Ireland's two governments. Added to this the apparent dislike of railways by the UTA, the writing was already on the wall for the CDRJC. A continued fall in traffic and receipts continued from 1955 to 1958, and by 1957 it was obvious that the CDRJC's days were numbered. A formal application was made to the Transport Tribunal to end services in 1959 and approval was given; the railway closed on 1 January 1960.

The County Donegal Railways Joint Committee also operated bus and road freight services from 1930. These were taken over by the GNR(I) in 1933 and lasted until 1955. From 1955, the CDRJC took over the services. These continued past the closure of the railway system until they were taken over by Córas Iompair Éireann (CIÉ) in 1971.

The Londonderry & Lough Swilly Railway had its beginnings with a broad-gauge line from Londonderry to Farland Point. From Farland Point, numerous small boats traversed Lough Swilly, connecting the various towns and villages. Another line was built from a junction with the existing line to Buncrana and Fahan Pier. The original Farland Point line was eventually closed. It was the promotion of the Letterkenny Railway that prompted the change to narrow gauge, the Letterkenny Railway being constructed to 3ft. gauge and the rest of the Lough Swilly being converted in 1885.

The passing of the Railways (Ireland) Act in 1896 saw the Lough Swilly expand. The government funded two lines, one from Buncrana to Carndonagh and the other from Letterkenny to Burtonport - known as the Letterkenny & Burtonport Extension Railway. With these two lines open, the company's route mileage increased to 99 miles. There was constant criticism of the way the Lough Swilly was run and two inquiries were held to investigate goings on. This eventually resulted in a change of management in 1917 and matters improved.

The period of the First World War saw the railway suffer as fish traffic dropped off. This was only made worse by partition in Ireland in 1922 and the resulting civil war in the Free State, the railway suffering numerous attacks. The finances of the company declined and, by 1925, liquid reserves had been exhausted. The railway approached the Free State government for a grant in 1924 and, after some deliberation, it was given. A similar grant from the Northern government was made from 1925.

With increasing competition from road transport, the Lough Swilly was finding it difficult to compete. As a result, the company decided that it would run its own bus and road freight services from 1929 and subsequently bought up numerous small concerns competing against it. As the bus operation became established, train services were reduced. The Buncrana—Carndonagh section was closed in 1935, with a limited service from Londonderry to Buncrana being operated. 1940 saw the Burtonport Extension lose its services entirely. The war years saw an increase in traffic, particularly as wartime restrictions of fuel began to have an effect. Buncrana enjoyed a full service from 1942 and the Burtonport extension saw the resumption of goods services in 1941 as far as Gweedore, the rest of the line having been lifted. Passengers were also carried from 1943. However, the post-war period saw a decline and passenger services were discontinued on the Burtonport Extension in 1947 and Buncrana in 1948. Full closure of the remaining lines came in 1953. The Lough Swilly continued as a bus company, running extensive services throughout Co. Donegal.

Acknowledgements

The publishers wish to thank the following for contributing photographs to this book. John Alsop for pages 13 and 25-27; Richard Casserley for the front cover, inside front cover, pages 5-11, 14, 15 (both), 18, 21-24, 28, 30-36, 38-41, 43-48, the inside back cover and the back cover; Lawrence Morrison for pages 1, 29, 37 and 42.

Strabane to Killybegs

Passenger service withdrawn	1 January 1960
Distance	50 miles
Company	County Donegal Railways Joint Committee

Stations closed	Date
Strabane	1 January 1960
Clady	1 January 1960
Castlefinn	1 January 1960
Liscooly	1 January 1960
Killygordon	1 January 1960
Cavan Halt	1 January 1960
County Home Gate	1956
Town Bridge Halt	c.1950
Stranorlar	1 January 1960
Meenglas Halt	1 January 1960
Derg Bridge Halt	1 January 1960
Barnesmore Halt *	1 January 1960
Lough Eske **	1 January 1960
Harvey's Hill	1944
Clar Bridge Halt ***	1 January 1960
Donegal	1 January 1960
Drimark Hill	1956
Killymard Halt	1956 (used for special occasions only until 1960)
Mountcharles	1 January 1960
Doorin Road Halt	1 January 1960
Mullanboy Halt	1 January 1960
Inver Church	1 January 1960
Inver	1 January 1960
Port	1 January 1960
Dunkineely	1 January 1960
Spamount	1 January 1960
Bruckless	1 January 1960
Ardara Road	1 January 1960
Killybegs	1 January 1960

* Formerly Barrack Bridge Halt.
** Named Druminin until 1889.
*** Formerly Clar.

Strabane in neighbouring Co. Tyrone had got a railway in 1847 when the Londonderry & Enniskillen Railway (L&ER) opened their line from Londonderry. It wasn't long before landowners in Co. Donegal thought about providing a connection to Strabane and on 15 May 1860, an Act was received authorising the Finn Valley Railway (FVR) to build a 14-mile line from Strabane to Stranorlar. Funds proved difficult to raise and a loan from the Public Works Loan Commissioners enabled the line to be built, opening for traffic on 7 September 1863. Built to the Irish broad gauge of 5ft 3in., it was worked by the L&ER's successor, the Irish North Western Railway (INWR). Stations were provided at Clady, Castlefinn, Liscooly and Killygordon.

Railcar No. 10 at Strabane, Co. Tyrone, with the 9.55 a.m. service to Stranorlar, 21 September 1953.

The final evolution of the CDR railcars were in the form of Nos. 19 and 20, built by Walker Brothers in 1950. Here, No. 19 is at Clady with the 11.10 a.m. service between Strabane and Stranorlar, 19 May 1950.

Further expansion was considered and a separate company was set up, the West Donegal Railway (WDR), receiving an Act on 21 July 1879 to build a 3ft gauge railway from Stranorlar to Donegal. Work on the narrow-gauge line commenced, but funds ran out before Donegal was reached, the line only getting as far as Druminin (later called Lough Eske), some four miles short of Donegal Town. However, the rolling stock arrived in 1882 and services from Stranorlar to Druminin commenced on 25 April that year. This led to a peculiar situation as the WDR was worked by the FVR, who in turn was now worked by the INWR's successor, the Great Northern Railway of Ireland (GNR(I))!

The same date and the same train at Claddy, but facing in the opposite direction. Both Nos. 19 and 20 were sold to the Isle of Man Railway in 1961, where they still survive.

Donegal town was finally reached seven years later with services commencing on 1 September 1889. However, although the WDR finally managed to complete the line, they did not have enough money to build the station, which was constructed by a separate company and leased back to the WDR. On opening, only stations at Druminin and Donegal were provided. During the years leading up to the opening of the Killybegs extension, further stations were added along the route with Druminin being renamed Lough Eske in 1889. 1891 saw additional stops provided at Meenglas Halt, Barrack Bridge Halt (later renamed Barnesmore Halt) and Clar (later Clar Bridge Halt).

Class 5 2-6-4T No. 5, built by Nasmyth, Wilson in 1907 and named 'Drumboe', at Castlefinn with the 12.45 p.m. service between Stranorlar and Strabane, 20 April 1948.

Further extension of the WDR to Killybegs was assisted by the passing of the Light Railways (Ireland) Act of 1889. Under the provisions of this Act, a certain amount of state aid was available so advantage was taken of this and the WDR commenced work on the extension. In the meantime, the associated FVR had received funding for a narrow-gauge extension to Glenties. As a result of the expansion of the system, the two nominally separate concerns received government approval to merge to form the Donegal Railway Company in June 1892. In addition, the FVR line from Strabane to Stranorlar was given permission in 1893 to re-gauge from 5ft 3in. to 3ft gauge. The FVR had been renting station space from the GNR(I) at Strabane and further approval

Class 5 2-6-4T No. 8, 'Foyle', at Castlefinn with the 1.05 p.m. service between Donegal and Londonderry, 23 June 1937.

was given for the new Donegal Railway to make its own approach via a new bridge over the River Mourne to a new narrow-gauge terminal adjacent to the GNR(I) station. In the meantime, the Killybegs extension had been completed and opened for traffic on 18 August 1893. Nearly a year later, over the weekend of 13—15 July 1894, the former FVR Strabane—Stranorlar section was re-gauged and the new narrow-gauge station at Strabane was opened at the same time. Seven stations were provided on the extension at Mountcharles, Doorin Road, Inver, Port, Dunkineely, Bruckless and Ardara Road.

Walker Brothers articulated railcar No. 12 at Dunkineely with the 1.37 p.m. service between Donegal and Killybegs, 21 April 1953.

As operations continued, a further stop was added at Killymard in 1895. Transition to joint ownership by the English Midland Railway and GNR(I) did not have too much affect on operations, but an additional stop was added at Derg Bridge Halt on 2 December 1912. The First World War saw a number of stations closed, including Meenglas Halt and Killymard Halt, in August 1918. The introduction of internal combustion powered railcars in the 1920s, which were able to stop virtually anywhere, saw a number of additional stopping places being added over the years. Cavan Halt and Mullanaboy Halt were added in 1931, Town Bridge Halt in 1934, Inver Church in 1936, while Meenglas Halt and Killymard Halt were reopened in 1936. County Home Gate, Drimark Hill, Spamount and Harvey's Hill opened in 1944, although the latter closed the same year. In addition to these stops, a number of level crossings along the line were also advertised as railcar stops, most being added between 1936 and 1944.

Railcar No. 12 at Killybegs with the 3.50 p.m. service to Donegal, 21 April 1953. No. 12 is now preserved in full working order on the Foyle Valley Railway, Londonderry.

The town and station of Killybegs.

The Second World War and coal shortages of 1944 and 1947 did not have too much effect on the line, but post-war road competition began to make inroads. A number of station closures were made including Town Bridge Halt in 1950, and County Home Gate and Drimark Hill in 1956. Killymard Halt also closed in 1956 but remained in use for occasional special traffic.

Class 2 4-6-0T No. 4, 'Meenglas', stands at Killybegs Shed. Built by Neilson it was withdrawn in 1935.

However, the writing was on the wall and a number of line closures had already taken place elsewhere on the system. The Strabane—Killybegs line closed for passenger traffic on 1 January 1960. Freight services on the Strabane—Stranorlar section continued a few weeks longer until complete closure came on 25 January 1960.

Strabane to Killybegs

Stranorlar to Glenties

Passenger service withdrawn	15 December 1947
Distance	24 miles
Company	County Donegal Railways Joint Committee

Stations closed	Date
Stranorlar	1 January 1960
Ballybofey	15 December 1947
Ballindoon Bridge	15 December 1947
Glenmore	15 December 1947
Cloghan	15 December 1947
Elatagh Halt	15 December 1947

Stations closed	Date
Cronadun Bridge	15 December 1947
Glassagh Halt	15 December 1947
Ballinamore	15 December 1947
Fintown *	Open
Shallogans Halt	15 December 1947
Glenties	15 December 1947

* Fintown closed 15 December 1947, but reopened 3 June 1996 as part of the Cumann na Gaeltachta Láir preservation project.

The Finn Valley Railway (FVR) received funding to make an extension from Stranorlar to Glenties following the route of the River Finn. The passing of the Light Railways (Ireland) Act of 1889 enabled the company to receive state aid to build the line. However, the extension was to be built to 3ft narrow gauge whereas the rest of the FVR line from Strabane was 5ft 3in. broad gauge. In 1892 the West Donegal and Finn Valley Railways were given permission to merge to form the Donegal Railway and the following year saw authorisation given to re-gauge the Strabane—Stranorlar section to 3ft narrow gauge.

Stranorlar Station, 20 April 1948.

14　　Stranorlar to Glenties

Stranorlar Station, looking west, 20 April 1948.

Stranorlar Station, looking east, 20 April 1948.

Stranorlar Station.

Construction commenced and the 24-mile line was completed and was opened for traffic on 3 June 1895 by the newly formed Donegal Railway. Stations were provided at Ballybofey, Glenmore, Cloghan, Ballinamore and Fintown. In 1911 the additional stop of Shallogan's Halt was opened, three miles from the terminus at Glenties. The introduction of railcars saw new stops being provided with Elatagh Halt opening in 1930 and Ballindoon Bridge and Cronadun Bridge in 1944. As was usual with the County Donegal, the introduction of railcars saw additional stops being provided at a number of level crossings along the line.

The first of the full width cab railcars, Nos. 15 and 16, built by Walker Brothers and the GNR(I), at Stranorlar, 1954.

Railcar No. 10 with trailer No. 2 entering Stranorlar, 20 April 1948. Originally built for the Clogher Valley Railway by Walker Brothers in 1932, the railcar was acquired by the CDR in 1941 following the closure of the CVR.

Competition from road transport affected this line at an early stage with passenger and goods services being discontinued on 15 December 1947. The line continued in use for a few more years with occasional livestock and turf trains, the turf - or peat - being produced at the Turf Development Board's (Bord na Móna from 1946) bog at Glenties. However, these were discontinued on 19 September 1949 with line lying derelict until complete closure came a few years later on 10 March 1952.

Railcars Nos. 3 and 15, and Class 4 4-6-4T No. 15, 'Mourne', at Stranorlar works and shed, 16 August 1938. Railcar No. 3 was acquired from the Dublin & Blessington Steam Tramway and re-gauged from 5ft. 3in. to 3ft. Rebuilt as a trailer in 1944, No. 3 survives in the Ulster Folk and Transport Museum.

Cloghan Station, Ballybofey.

The story doesn't end here though. In 1995 a preservation group, Cumann na Gaeltachta Láir, reopened Fintown Station. The group have also relaid some track from the station westwards along the banks of Lough Finn towards Glenties.

Donegal to Ballyshannon

Passenger service withdrawn	1 January 1960	*Stations closed*	*Date*
Distance	15 miles	Drumhorry Bridge	1 January 1960
Company	County Donegal Railways Joint Committee	Ballintra	1 January 1960
		Dromore Halt	1 January 1960
Stations closed	*Date*	Dorrian's Bridge	1 January 1960
Donegal	1 January 1960	Rossnowlagh	1 January 1960
Hospital Halt	*c.*1950	Friary Halt	1 January 1960
Drumbar Halt	1 January 1960	Coolmore Halt	1 January 1960
Laghey	1 January 1960	Creevy Halt	1 January 1960
Bridgetown	1 January 1960	Ballyshannon	1 January 1960

Donegal Station, looking east, 21 April 1953.

Donegal Station, 21 April 1953.

The town of Ballyshannon was put on the railway map in 1866 when the Bundoran Junction—Bundoran line was opened by the Enniskillen, Bundoran & Sligo Railway. However, in 1896 the Donegal Railway Act provided for two extensions to the Donegal Railway. One was from Strabane to Londonderry (see *Lost Railways of Co. 'Derry*) and the other to Ballyshannon. Unlike the other lines looked at so far, the Ballyshannon extension did not attract any state funding as the government didn't consider the area being served to be sufficiently impoverished to warrant state aid. As a result, it took some time to raise funds to build the line. The powers of the original Act eventually expired and new powers had to be obtained for the building of the Ballyshannon line, being received on 23 June 1902. The Act also authorised the purchase of the Donegal Station Company. Construction eventually started and the line was completed and opened for goods on 2 September 1905; passenger services followed on 21 September.

Ballyshannon Station, 21 April 1953.

Stations at Laghey, Bridgetown, Ballintra and Rossnowlagh were provided. In 1906 the Donegal Railway was taken over by the English Midland Railway and the Great Northern Railway of Ireland, forming the County Donegal Railways Joint Committee. That year the new ownership opened an additional stop, Drumbar Halt, just under two miles from Donegal. Another halt, Creevy Halt, near Ballyshannon, opened on 1 August 1911. In 1929 Coolmore Halt

Railcar No. 14 with trailer No. 6 and van No. 99, forming the 7.35 a.m. service to Donegal, at Ballyshannon, 21 April 1953.

opened, followed by Dromore Halt in 1930. The introduction of railcars saw additional stops being provided at Hospital Halt near Donegal Town in 1935 and at various level crossings from 1938 to 1940, including Dorrian's Bridge. Drumhorry Bridge was added in 1942 with Friary Halt opening in 1953. In the meantime, Hospital Halt had closed in 1950. The line was closed completely on 1 January 1960.

Strabane to Letterkenny

Passenger service withdrawn	1 January 1960	*Stations closed*	*Date*
Distance	19 miles	Coolaghy Halt	1 January 1960
Company	Strabane & Letterkenny Railway	Raphoe	1 January 1960
		Convoy	1 January 1960
Stations closed	*Date*	Cornagillagh Halt	1 January 1960
Strabane	1 January 1960	Glenmaquin	1 January 1960
Lifford Halt	1 January 1960	Letterkenny	1 January 1960
Ballindrait	1 January 1960		

Strabane Station in the mid-1950s as seen from the locomotive sheds. The signal cabin is on the GNR(I) broad gauge line and broad gauge wagons can be seen in the middle distance. The CDR station is to the right of the broad gauge wagons with a railcar in residence.

In the 1860s a proposal was made for a line from Letterkenny to Londonderry joining the Londonderry & Enniskillen Railway near St Johnstown. In the event a different proposal saw a line being built from Letterkenny to Londonderry by a more northerly route via Tooban by the Londonderry & Lough Swilly Railway. In 1903 the Strabane, Raphoe & Convoy Railway was promoted but, with the support of the Great Northern Railway of Ireland (GNR(I)), permission was given in 1904 to extend the route to Letterkenny and change the name to the Strabane & Letterkenny Railway (S&LR). Promoted as an

Strabane Station, looking west, 30 June 1937.

independent company, most of the financial backing came from the English Midland Railway and the GNR(I). The line was duly built and opened for traffic on 1 January 1909. It was worked by the County Donegal Railways Joint Committee (CDRJC) and the addition of this line effectively made the CDRJC the largest narrow-gauge system in Ireland with 124 route miles.

Strabane to Letterkenny

Strabane Station.

The line left Strabane and roughly followed a north-westerly route to Letterkenny with stations at Lifford, Ballindrait, Coolaghy Halt, Raphoe, Convoy and Glenmaquin. At Letterkenny, the S&LR crossed over the Lough Swilly line before terminating at a station adjacent to the Lough Swilly station. A siding connection was provided and a mount of traffic was exchanged between the companies. In 1911 an additional stop was provided, Cornagillagh Halt.

Railcar No. 20 with the 11.20 a.m. service to Letterkenny, 20 April 1953.

The shed at Letterkenny Station.

The introduction of railcars on the line saw additional stops being added in 1936 and 1944 at four level crossings along the line. Despite the economies of diesel railcars, road transport gradually overtook the railway and it closed on 1 January 1960, having remained nominally independent throughout its life.

Tooban Junction to Burtonport

Passenger service withdrawn   Tooban Junction—Letterkenny: 1 July 1953;
Letterkenny—Gweedore: 6 January 1947;
Gweedore—Burtonport: 3 July 1940

Distance   68 miles

Company   Londonderry & Lough Swilly Railway /
Letterkenny & Burtonport Extension Railway

Stations closed

Station	Date
Tooban Junction *	1 July 1953
Trady	1866
Carrowen	1 July 1953
Newtoncunningham	1 July 1953
Sallybrook	1 July 1953
Manorcunningham	1 July 1953
Pluck	1 July 1953
Letterkenny	1 July 1953
Old Town	6 January 1947
Newmills	6 January 1947
Foxhall	6 January 1947
Churchhill	6 January 1947
Kilmacrenan	6 January 1947
Barnes Halt	1940
Creeslough	6 January 1947
Dunfanaghy Road	6 January 1947
Falcarragh	6 January 1947
Cashelnagore	6 January 1947
Gweedore	6 January 1947
Crolly	3 July 1940
Kincasslagh Road	3 July 1940
Dungloe **	3 July 1940
Burtonport	3 July 1940

* Formerly called Junction; closed July 1866. Reopened as Burnfoot Junction in 1883 and renamed Tooban Junction in 1920.
** Formerly Loughmeela, Dungloe Road (Loughmeela), Dungloe (Loughmeela) and finally Dungloe.

Carrowen Station, 20 April 1953.

4-6-2T No. 15, built by Hudswell, Clarke in 1899, at Newtoncunningham with the 2.15 p.m. service between Letterkenny and Londonderry, 20 April 1953.

On 26 June 1853 Parliament authorised the Lough Foyle & Lough Swilly Railway to build a line from Londonderry to Farland Point on the shores of Lough Swilly. A pier at Farland Point served various small shipping links to various towns and villages along the shore. The company changed its name to the Londonderry & Lough Swilly Railway (L&LSR) during the passage of the Bill through parliament in 1853, but it took until 1860 (with an additional Act in 1859) before construction started. Opening on 31 December 1863, the line was built to the Irish broad gauge of 5ft 3in. The line left Londonderry from the company's Graving Dock terminus, running north-west to Tooban before turning south-west to Farland Point. Stations were provided at Gallagh

Sallybrook Station, 20 April 1953.

Road, Bridge End and Trady. Another Act of 1861 authorised the L&LSR to extend their line to Buncrana, some 12 miles north of Londonderry. The Buncrana line left the existing railway at a junction near Tooban, simply called Junction. Opening in 1864, an additional station was provided at Harrity's Road as well as Junction. The opening of the Buncrana line left the original Farland Point line as a branch. It ended up being worked by horses for a period in early 1865 before reverting back to steam locomotives. However, poor performance of the line resulted in its closure in June 1866. The track was lifted in 1877 and that seemed to be the end of the line.

The 2.15 p.m. service from Letterkenny at Manorcunningham Station, 20 April 1953.

The Letterkenny Railway (LR) was authorised in 1860 to build a line from Letterkenny to the Londonderry & Enniskillen Railway near St Johnstown. However, another Act of 1863 allowed the company to alter its route and to make a junction with the L&LSR's Buncrana line. Although work commenced, funds ran out in 1865 and it took until 1880, and another three Acts, before another Act was passed allowing the Letterkenny Railway to build the line as a 3ft narrow-gauge line with the financial assistance of a Baronial Guarantee (the change of gauge was a condition of the financial aid). The same Act also allowed the L&LSR to change their gauge. Construction recommenced and the line was built to connect with the L&LSR at Junction Station, which when reopened became known as Burnfoot Junction (for a while it was a mixed gauge station with the narrow gauge terminating there). In point of fact, the

L&LSR engine No. 15 with the 2.15 p.m. service to Londonderry at Letterkenny Station, 20 April 1953.

LR was responsible for the line only as far as Burt Junction, near Trady, and the L&LSR was responsible from Burt Junction to Burnfoot Junction. There was no junction as such at Burt; the line was continuous throughout and it simply marked the point between one company and another. After more financial difficulties were resolved with a loan from the Board of Works, the line eventually opened on 30 June 1883, being worked by the L&LSR. The LR was soon in more financial trouble by 1887 when it was unable to pay the interest on the Board of Works loan. As a result, the company was taken over by the Board of Works and the L&LSR continued to work it.

Kilmacrenan Station.

The L&LSR had shown an interest in extending their system to both the north and west, planning a line to Dunfanaghy in 1885. Further to the west lay the small fishing town of Burtonport. In an effort to alleviate poverty in this remote part of Donegal, the government had paid for a harbour to be built, the only problem being that there was no effective communication to the town. In 1896 the Railways (Ireland) Act was passed, allowing central government to give grants for the construction of railways to underdeveloped and impoverished areas. Two years later plans were put forward for a line

Kilmacrenan Station, looking south, 23 June 1937.

from Letterkenny to Burtonport and were approved as the Letterkenny & Burtonport Extension Railway. With the aid of a £300,000 grant, construction commenced, crossing some of the most remote and bleak countryside in Ireland. Despite the enormous size of the grant, the line ended up costing more, the deficit being made up by a £5,000 Baronial Guarantee.

Creeslough Station.

Opening for traffic on 9 March 1903, the Letterkenny & Burtonport Extension Railway (L&BER) was a separate company worked by the L&LSR. The line carried on from Letterkenny with stations provided at Old Town, New Mills, Foxhall, Churchhill, Kilmacrenan, Creeslough, Dunfanaghy Road, Falcarragh, Cashelnagore, Gweedore, Crolly and Dungloe. The line required some major engineering features, including three major viaducts at Barnes Gap, Faymore and Owencarrow. The latter was particularly impressive, being some 380 yards long and 50 feet high. Additional stations were provided at Kincasslagh Road in 1913 and Barnes Halt in 1927. In the meantime, Burnfoot Junction was renamed Tooban Junction in 1920.

No. 12, one of the pair of 4-8-0 tender engines built by Hudswell, Clarke in 1905, at Gweedore Station with the 8.30 a.m. service from Burtonport, 24 June 1937.

Part of the grant had paid for locomotives and rolling stock and led to an interesting situation. It was a condition of the grant that L&BER locomotives carried the L&BER letters on the side and were numbered in their own sequence to distinguish them from the L&LSR locomotives. Furthermore, L&BER locomotives were not to be used elsewhere on the system. In the event, the locomotives carried L&LSR numbers and were used elsewhere, resulting in arguments with the Board of Works.

Gweedore Station, 24 June 1937.

The line was not without other difficulties and in 1906 a train was blown off the exposed Owencarrow Viaduct during a gale. The same thing happened again in 1925, this time killing four passengers. Government enquiries were held in 1905 and again in 1917 to investigate allegations that the line was badly and unsafely worked. The latter enquiry saw the resignation of the L&LSR chairman and a new management installed, improving matters considerably. One of the features of the L&BER were the locomotives provided to work the line. Although the initial order was for four 4-6-0Ts, their limited coal and water capacity led to an order for further locomotives. The first order from Hudswell, Clarke of Leeds, delivered in 1905, was for two 4-8-0 tender locomotives. This was followed in 1912 by two 4-8-4T tanks from the same builder, the largest tank locomotives to work on a British narrow gauge system.

Gweedore Station, 24 June 1937.

Partition in 1922, and the subsequent amalgamations in Éire in 1924, were serious blows to the company. Operating in both Northern Ireland and Éire meant that the company was not eligible for amalgamation into the Great Southern Railways and so it remained independent. Traffic flowing between the two countries was subject to customs examinations with all the attendant delays. Furthermore, the natural traffic flow from Donegal was to Londonderry. With partition, this flow was disrupted with traffic now being forwarded to the established markets in the south. The company began losing money from 1925 and was kept solvent by grants from both governments. In the meantime, the L&LSR started to run bus and road freight services in the

Tooban Junction to Burtonport

Hudswell, Clarke 4-8-0 No. 12 with the 8.30 a.m. service to Londonderry at Burtonport Station, 24 June 1937.

county. With a contraction of the railway business and an expansion of the bus operation, it was inevitable that closures would take place. In 1940 the entire line from Tooban Junction to Burtonport was closed to passengers on 3 July, with the Letterkenny to Burtonport section closing completely. However, road-based public transport was beginning to suffer from Emergency Restrictions due to the Second World War. The goods service was restored on 3 February 1941, but only as far as Gweedore. The Gweedore to Burtonport section had already been lifted! From March 1942 limited passenger accommodation was provided on trains. This proved to be short lived for on 6 January 1947 the Letterkenny to Gweedore section was closed again, although a few specials ran up until June 1947.

Burtonport shed.

Freight traffic survived to Letterkenny for another few years until that was discontinued and the line from Tooban Junction to Letterkenny closed completely on 1 July 1953. The remainder of the line from Tooban Junction to Londonderry closed with the Buncrana line on 9 August 1953.

Tooban Junction to Carndonagh

Passenger service withdrawn — Tooban Junction to Buncrana: 10 August 1953; Buncrana to Carndonagh: 2 December 1935

Distance — 24 miles

Company — Londonderry & Lough Swilly Railway

Stations closed	Date
Tooban Junction *	10 August 1953
Inch Road	10 August 1953
Lamberton's Halt	1948
Fahan	10 August 1953
Beach Halt	c.1948
Lisfannon Golf Links **	1948
Buncrana	10 August 1953
Ballymagan	2 December 1935
Kinnego Halt	2 December 1935
Drumfries	2 December 1935
Meendoran Halt	2 December 1935
Clonmany	2 December 1935
Ballyliffin	2 December 1935
Rashenny	2 December 1935
Carndoagh Halt	2 December 1935
Carndonagh	2 December 1935

* Formely called Junction; closed July 1866. Reopened as Burnfoot Junction in 1883 and renamed Tooban Junction in 1920.

** Formerly Golf Halt; renamed 1922.

Tooban Junction Station, 20 April 1953.

4-6-0T No. 3, built by Andrew Barclay in 1902, at Tooban Junction.
The 2.15 p.m. service from Letterkenny is on the left, 20 April 1953.

The first part of the history of this line from Londonderry to Burnfoot Junction has been described in the previous chapter. It was the Act of July 1861 that authorised the Londonderry & Lough Swilly Railway (L&LSR) to extend their line from the Farland Point line at the location that simply became known as Junction. Opening for traffic on 8 September 1864, the broad-gauge line took over in importance from the Farland Point line for the time being. Stations were provided at Inch Road and Fahan. A short spur left the line to Fahan Pier.

Tooban Junction, 20 April 1953.

It was the building of the Letterkenny Railway and the Act of 1880 that prompted the conversion of the line from broad gauge to 3ft narrow gauge. In the event, the line was not converted until 28 March 1885. The arrival of the Letterkenny Railway saw the former Junction Station reopen as Burnfoot Junction. The golf club at Lisfannon received a halt in 1892 called Golf Halt (renamed as Lisfannon Golf Links in 1922).

Buncrana Station, 15 April 1948.

In 1884 the L&LSR had shown an interest in extending the line from Buncrana to Carndonagh. However, it took until the passing of the Railways (Ireland) Act of 1896 before plans were revived. The Act made for the provision of grants to be given to construct railways to underdeveloped and impoverished areas. Although a grant of nearly £100,000 was given to build the extension, a £5,000 deficit on costs had to be made up by the L&LSR by means of a Baronial Guarantee. Opening for traffic on 1 July 1901, the line continued north through Ballymagan, Drumfries, Meendoran Halt, Clonmany and Ballyliffin before turning south-east through Rashenny to Carndonagh.

Tooban Junction to Carndonagh

4-6-2T No. 10, built by Kerr, Stuart in 1904, with the 5.07 p.m. service to Londonderry at Buncrana, 19 April 1948.

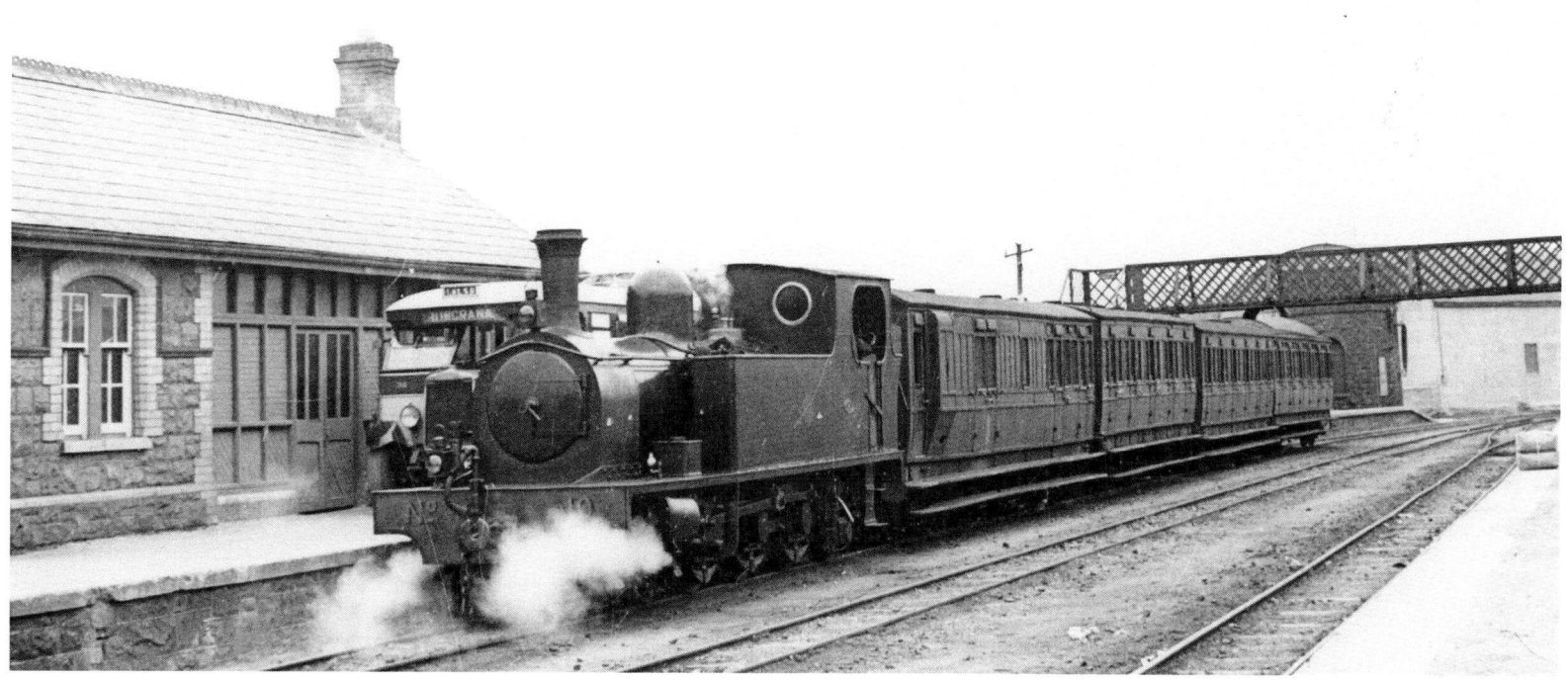

As the government had paid for the railway, certain restrictions applied over the use of locomotives. The locomotives bought for the Carndonagh extension were only meant to be used on that line. Needless to say, these locomotives could be found working the Letterkenny section and at one point the Board of Works took the L&LSR to task over it.

4-6-2T No. 10, formerly named 'Richmond', at Buncrana with the 5.07 p.m. service to Londonderry, 19 April 1948.

As with the Burtonport extension, partition in 1922 caused major problems for the L&LSR with customs examinations. The company began to lose money in 1925 and had to be financially supported by the country's two governments. An additional stop was provided at Lamberton's Halt in 1927, although the company began to expand into providing bus and road freight services in the area in 1929. Three additional halts were opened in 1930 at Kinnego Halt, Meendoran Halt and Carndoagh Halt. With the bus services becoming established and the railway increasingly more expensive to run, train services from Buncrana to Carndonagh were reduced severely in 1931, with just two trains a week. However, the local roads were not up to the traffic and services had to be restored again three months later. However, the situation continued to decline on the railway and on 2 December 1935 the Buncrana to Carndonagh section closed completely. Buncrana was left with a limited summer service.